MW00676708

Cora Alexander

Maria Lomeli Padilla

November 2006

THE BOOK OF
BLESSINGS

Honor Books

07 06 05 04 03   10 9 8 7 6 5 4 3 2 1

The Book of Blessings
ISBN 1-56292-418-4

Copyright © 2003 by **Bordon Books**
6532 E. 71 Street, Suite 105
Tulsa, OK 74133

Published by Honor Books,
An Imprint of Cook Communications Ministries
4050 Lee Vance View
Colorado Springs, CO 80918

Developed by Borbon Books

Manuscript written and compiled by Betsy Williams, Tulsa, Oklahoma.

INTRODUCTION

You are blessed! But we all know how easy it is to take for granted the many blessings with which we have been endowed. It's hard to count blessings when you can hardly keep track of all your daily appointments; but, yes, you have been blessed in many different ways by a God who gets a kick out of doing wonderful things for you. Family, a place to sleep at night, food on the table, friends, kind words spoken at important moments in your life, even that beautiful sunset last night—these are some of the many ways that God says, "I love you. I care about you."

Take a moment now and enjoy this collection of quotations, prayers, poems, and meditations on the blessings of life. Turn the pages and remember the ways in which God's blessings have already made your life abundant and good. And those special friends and loved ones in your life? Included are prayers of blessing that you can pray over them.

While you are reflecting on the wonderful things in your life, don't forget to remind yourself that you are loved very much by Someone who loves to shower you with blessings.

May the blessings of light be upon you,
Light without and light within.
And in all your comings and goings,
May you ever have a kindly greeting
From them you meet along the road.

Deep peace of the running waves to you.
Deep peace of the flowing air to you.
Deep peace of the smiling stars to you.
Deep peace of the quiet earth to you.
Deep peace of the watching
shepherds to you.
Deep peace of the Son of Peace to you.

There's a special kind of freedom friends enjoy:
freedom to share innermost thoughts,
to ask a favor, to show their true feelings—
the freedom to simply be themselves.

**Friendship improves happiness, and
abates misery, by doubling our joy,
and dividing our grief.**

In poverty and any other misfortunes of life,
true friends are a sure refuge. The young
they keep out of mischief; the old they comfort
and aid in their weakness; and those in the
prime of life they incite to noble deeds.

*Two are better than one,
because they have a good return for their work:
If one falls down,
his friend can help him up.*
ECCLESIASTES 4:9–10 NIV

YOU ARE BLESSED WITH FRIENDS!

A blessed thing is for any man
or woman to have a friend:
one human soul whom we can trust utterly:
who knows the best and the worst of us,
and who loves us in spite of all our faults;
who will speak the honest truth to us,
while the world flatters us to our face,
and laughs at us behind our back;
who will give us counsel and reproof in the
day of prosperity and self-conceit,
but who, again, will comfort and encourage
us in the day of difficulty and sorrow,
when the world leaves us alone to fight our
own battle as we can.

A true friend is always loyal, and
a brother is born to help in time of need.

PROVERBS 17:17

After the friendship of God,
a friend's affection is the
greatest treasure here below.

**A friend is one who
knows you as you are,
understands where you've been,
accepts who you've become,
and still gently invites you to grow.**

Friendship is like a garden. It thrives under
little daily attentions: a weed pulled here,
the earth loosened there. Do you have friends
you value? Send a card today telling them so.
If their lives are a blessing to you, turn
around and bless them by letting them know.

A PRAYER OF BLESSING FOR A FRIEND

May God bless you, my wonderful friend! May you know how special you are to me and how thankful I am for your friendship. May the joy you bring to others be returned to you many times over, and may you experience life in all its fullness.

May your relationships be rich and meaningful, and may you never know loneliness. May God comfort you in times of sadness and grief, so sorrow cannot overtake you. May you be kept from all harm and be blessed with good health. May your life be a long one, surpassing your expectations.

May you never know lack but have all your needs met. Instead of being seized by fear during difficult times, may you take refuge next to God's heart. May you be wise in your decisions and discerning in all your ways. May you experience success in everything you do.

Most of all may you realize how precious you are to God. He loves you so much that He continually thinks of you, and I believe you bring a smile to His face. Regardless of the challenges you face, may He work everything out for your good and give you peace.

Amen.

COUNT YOUR MANY BLESSINGS

When upon life's billows you
are tempest tossed,

When you are discouraged,
thinking all is lost,

Count your many blessings,
name them one by one,

And it will surprise you what
the Lord hath done.

Are you ever burdened
with a load of care?

Does the cross seem heavy
you are called to bear?

Count your many blessings,
every doubt will fly,

And you will be singing as the days go by.

When you look at others
with their lands and gold,

Think that Christ has promised you
His wealth untold;

Count your many blessings,
money cannot buy

Your reward in heaven,
nor your home on high.

So, amid the conflict,
whether great or small,

Do not be discouraged, God is over all;

Count your many blessings,
angels will attend,

Help and comfort give you
to your journey's end.

A PASSAGE OF BLESSING FROM THE BIBLE

The Beatitudes

[Jesus] began to teach them, saying:
"Blessed are the poor in spirit,
for theirs is the kingdom of heaven.
Blessed are those who mourn,
for they will be comforted.
Blessed are the meek,
for they will inherit the earth.
Blessed are those who hunger
and thirst for righteousness,
for they will be filled.
Blessed are the merciful,
for they will be shown mercy.
Blessed are the pure in heart,
for they will see God.

Blessed are the peacemakers,
for they will be called sons of God.

Blessed are those who are persecuted
because of righteousness,
for theirs is the kingdom of heaven.

Blessed are you when people insult you,
persecute you and falsely say all kinds of evil against
you because of me. Rejoice and be glad, because
great is your reward in heaven, for in the same way
they persecuted the prophets who were before you."

MATTHEW 5:2–12 NIV

The religious system of Jesus' day
left out the multitudes, but Jesus
welcomed all into His kingdom.
Anyone could come. They still can.
That is the gospel of the Beatitudes.

All the days ordained for me
were written in your book
before one of them came to be.
PSALM 139:16 NIV

Believing hear, what you deserve to hear:
Your birthday as my own to me is dear.
Blessed and distinguished days,
which we should prize
The first, the kindest bounty of the skies.
But yours gives most; for mine did only lend
Me to the world; yours gave to me a friend.

Our birthdays are feathers
in the broad wing of time.

A PRAYER OF BLESSING FOR A BIRTHDAY

Happy birthday! May you be blessed today as we celebrate your life and what you mean to me! May it be a day as special as you are, filled with all of your favorite things, and may it be the beginning of the best year you've known yet.

May you put past adversity and pain behind you, while holding the memory of good things closely to your heart. May you look forward with anticipation to the days ahead, trusting that God is at work in your life to bless you.

May you experience wholeness and a sense of well-being in your spirit, your soul, and your body. May your heart be filled with God's love, and may that love fill any empty spot you feel inside. As you are filled to overflowing, may He use you to pass His love on to others.

May God's peace guard your mind to shield you from stress and fear, and may His joy fill your days with singing. And as you enjoy the warmth of His presence, may He grant you your heart's desire.

Amen.

Give thanks to the LORD, call on his name;
make known among the nations what he has done.
PSALM 105:1 NIV

Best of all is it to preserve everything in a pure,
still heart, and let there be for every pulse
a thanksgiving, and for every breath a song.

Thanksgiving is a good thing;
thanksliving is better.

Thankfulness causes a change in the heart,
and scientists tell us it changes our chemistry
for the better. Try it. Thank God for
ten blessings you now enjoy. Food? Home?
Friends? Do it slowly and meditatively,
realizing what life would be without
these ten blessings. There now. Feel better?

THE BLESSING OF GIVING THANKS

Of all the many, many gifts
We long so to possess,
The one that is the best is this,
The gift of thankfulness.

Of all the blessings we receive
Which happiness imparts,
The one which brings real joy is this,
Thanksgiving in the heart.

Sing out your thanks to him;
sing praises to our God.
PSALM 147:7

A prayer of blessing from the Bible:

Praise God, O world! May all the peoples
of the earth give thanks to you. For the earth
has yielded abundant harvests. God, even
our own God, will bless us. And peoples
from remotest lands will worship him.

PSALM 67:5–7

Observe God in His works: here fountains flow,
Birds sing, beasts feed, fish leap,
and th' earth stands fast:
Above are restless motions, running lights,
Vast circling azure, giddly clouds, days, nights.

One is nearer God's heart in a garden
Than anywhere else on earth.

A PASSAGE OF BLESSING FROM THE BIBLE

God Blessed Adam and Eve with Life!

God created people in his own image;
God patterned them after himself;
male and female he created them.

God blessed them and told them, "Multiply and
fill the earth and subdue it. Be masters over the fish
and birds and all the animals." And God said, "Look!
I have given you the seed-bearing plants throughout
the earth and all the fruit trees for your food. And
I have given all the grasses and other green plants to
the animals and birds for their food." And so it was.

GENESIS 1:27–30 NLT

O world, as God has made it!
All is beauty.

You may offer yeast bread and honey as thanksgiving offerings at harvest time.

LEVITICUS 2:12

When thankfulness overflows the swelling heart, and breathes in free and uncorrupted praise for blessings received, Heaven takes such acknowledgment as fragrant incense, and doubles all its blessings.

Just the word *thanksgiving* prompts the spirit of humility—genuine gratitude to God for His mercy, His abundance, His protection, His smile of favor. Life simplifies itself.

A PRAYER TO CELEBRATE OUR BLESSINGS ON THANKSGIVING DAY

Heavenly Father,

We set aside this day to honor You for Your many blessings. Thank You for inspiring the early settlers to establish our great land, so we can worship You in freedom. We cherish our liberty and praise You for it. May we never take it for granted.

We thank You for the blessing of our family and friends and the special place each person holds in our lives. We thank You for supplying all of our physical needs for food, shelter, and clothing and for doing so abundantly. Thank You that we never have to worry about these things, for You have promised to supply all of our needs.

Most of all, we bless You for satisfying the inner hunger in our hearts, for filling that place that only You can fill. We bless You for sending Your Son to die in our place so that we may live with You in Heaven forever. We bless You, Lord, with all of our hearts and dedicate this day to You.

Amen.

The heavens declare the glory of God;
the skies proclaim the work of his hands.

PSALM 19:1 NIV

May you understand the strength
and power of God
In a thunderstorm in Winter,
And the quiet beauty of creation,
In the calm of a Summer sunset.
And may you come to realize, that, insignificant
as you may seem in this great Universe,
You are an important part of God's plan.

May He watch over you and keep you safe from harm.

Have you taken the time to notice a sunset lately?
Maybe this evening would be a good time to do so.
As you pause and drink in the beauty of it,
notice the variety of colors and the way your
Heavenly Father has painted the sky. Maybe
today's palette will be designed just for you!

The Blessing of a Sunset

Lovely, yes,
And oddly beautiful—
The blended colors
Of this sunset.
Effective, too,
That long thin streak
Of bright chrome yellow,
Whose edges now
Are faintly tinged
With copper hues.
But then,
Sunsets are sunsets,
And there will be
Many more.
For, after all,
I await the coming
Of the night;
For then,
I shall count the stars.

We can almost smell the aroma of God's
beauty in the fresh spring flowers.
His breath surrounds us in
the warm summer breezes.

A prayer of blessing from the Bible:

May the God of your fathers, the Almighty,
bless you with blessings of heaven above
and of the earth beneath . . . blessings of
the grain and flowers, blessings reaching
to the utmost bounds of the everlasting hills.
GENESIS 49:25–26

I, even I, am he who comforts you
and gives you all this joy.
ISAIAH 51:12

AN UNEXPECTED BLESSING

Kay looked out her mother's kitchen window as she packed away dishes, pots, and pans. It had been a long and difficult winter. Her mother's struggle with cancer and finally her death seemed to squeeze all the joy out of Kay. She took comfort in the sounds of her children playing, and their hugs offered her comfort in her grief.

The snow had melted weeks ago but left a look of death on all it had enveloped. A glimmer of color caught Kay's eye. Small glimpses of green shot out of her mother's flowerbed surrounding the old oak tree. *Mother's tulips!* Kay thought. *They are coming up.*

Excitement Kay had not experienced in months overcame her. She bounded outside and into the crisp, cold air. She needed a closer look. Hidden under the harshness of winter, the most beautiful life was returning to eventually bloom again. Kay's heart would also bloom again with joy. It was time to let go and let the spirit of God's joy live through her again.

Kay felt a tug. *I'm still here,* she felt the Lord say. Kay knew she could go forward with the same spirit that raised Christ from the dead resurrecting her joy and giving her peace to overcome her grief.

Yes, Mother's tulips were blooming—in Kay.

It is no small thing to be on terms
of friendship with God.

*Abraham trusted God, and the Lord
declared him good in God's sight, and
he was even called "the friend of God."*

JAMES 2:23

*The Lord spoke to Moses face to face,
as a man speaks to his friend.*

EXODUS 33:11

**As I walked, I pondered deeply all that
consecration might mean to my life and—I was
afraid. And then, above the noise and clatter
of the street traffic came to me the message:
"You can trust the Man who died for you."**

Have you ever taken time to go for a walk
with God? What better way to enjoy
the company of a trusted friend than to take
a stroll on a lovely day. Think about how
amazing it is that the Creator of the Universe
wants to be your friend! He's always available
and always interested in what's on your mind.

YOU ARE BLESSED WITH GOD'S FRIENDSHIP

This, this is the God we adore,
Our faithful, unchangeable friend.
Whose love is as great as His power,
And neither knows measure nor end.

*We rejoice in our wonderful new relationship
with God—all because of what our
Lord Jesus Christ has done in dying
for our sins—making us friends of God.*
ROMANS 5:11

A prayer of blessing from the Bible:

*May God's love and the Holy Spirit's
friendship be yours.*
2 CORINTHIANS 13:14

God is my helper. He is a friend of mine!
PSALM 54:4

I love to think of nature as an unlimited
broadcasting station through which God
speaks to us every hour if we will only tune in.

If you have never heard the mountains
singing, or seen the trees of the field
clapping their hands, do not think because
of that they don't. Ask God to open your
ears so you may hear it and your eyes so
you may see it, because, though few men
ever know it, they do, my friend, they do.

In spring I delight you,
In summer I cool you,
In autumn I feed you,
In winter I warm you.
—A TREE

BLESSINGS REVEALED IN NATURE

Grant me, O God, the power to see
In every rose, eternity.
In every bud, the coming day;
In every snow, the promised May;
In every storm the legacy
Of rainbows smiling down at me!

From the time the world was created, people have
seen the earth and sky and all that God made.
They can clearly see his invisible qualities—
his eternal power and divine nature.
ROMANS 1:20 NLT

You know the familiar cliché: take time to
smell the roses. Busy, stressful lives prevent
us from even thinking about it, yet it is so
refreshing to take a minute and become aware of
one's surroundings. Tune in to that bird singing.
Take a long hard look at the vivid colors of the
flowers and trees. Take a slow, deep breath
and fill your senses with the aroma of nature.
Ahhh. Aren't you glad you did!

A rose can say I love you,
Orchids can enthrall,
But a weed bouquet in a chubby fist,
Oh my, that says it all!

**Children must be valued as our
most priceless possession.**

*Children are a gift from the LORD;
they are a reward from him.*
PSALM 127:3 NLT

A PARENT'S BLESSING ON THEIR CHILD

May God bless you and keep you safe in all of your comings and goings. May His goodness and mercy be your constant companions; and may you grow up strong, healthy, and wise. May He grant you grace in every challenge you face and confidence that He will see you through.

May God bless the works of your hands and mind so that everything you do will prosper. And in that prosperity may you always remember that every blessing comes from Him. May you always choose the right way, and may your heart be kind, filled with compassion and mercy.

In the future, may you be blessed with a spouse who honors and loves you. May your children and your children's children bless you and follow your example as You walk with God. But above all, may you be the kind of person who, all your life long, enjoys the companionship of God, and may He delight in your company, both now and throughout eternity.

Amen.

I love little children, and it is
not a slight thing
when they who are fresh
from God, love us.

We can't form our children
on our own concepts;
we must take them and love
them as God gives them to us.

We begin by imagining that
we are giving to them;
we end by realizing that they
have enriched us.

Children are God's apostles,
sent forth, day by day,
to preach of love, and hope and peace.

A PASSAGE OF BLESSING FROM THE BIBLE

Jesus Blessed the Little Children

*People were bringing little children to Jesus to have
him touch them, but the disciples rebuked them.
When Jesus saw this, he was indignant.
He said to them, "Let the little children come to me,
and do not hinder them, for the kingdom of God
belongs to such as these. I tell you the truth, anyone
who will not receive the kingdom of God like a little
child will never enter it." And he took the children
in his arms, put his hands on them and blessed them.*
MARK 10:13–16 NIV

The most eloquent prayer is the prayer
through hands that heal and bless.

*"The man who uses well what he is given shall
be given more, and he shall have abundance."*
MATTHEW 25:29

*Yes, God will give you much so that you can
give away much, and when we take your gifts
to those who need them they will break out into
thanksgiving and praise to God for your help.*
2 CORINTHIANS 9:11

The family that perseveres in good works
will surely have an abundance of blessings.

**The human contribution is the essential
ingredient. It is only in the giving
of oneself to others that we truly live.**

Have you ever had a secret pal, someone
for whom you do special things without their
knowledge? Think about the people you know.
Who could use a pick-me-up, a little extra
encouragement? Why not make an anonymous
card on your computer and drop it in the mail.
Who knows; you might be the source of that extra
umph to get them over the top. After all, friends
are definitely blessings that need to be cultivated.

THE BLESSING OF GENEROSITY

If you find that life is flat,
Full of this, with none of that,
Try giving!
Introspection makes it flatter;
A few more years—what will it matter?
Try giving!
If the world is dark and bitter;
Things all tend to make a quitter—
Try giving!
Forget yourself in helping others;
Know that all men are your brothers,
You will see then life is sweeter
Than you thought, and far completer—
When you give!

"If you give, you will receive. Your gift will return to
you in full measure, pressed down, shaken together
to make room for more, and running over."

LUKE 6:38 NLT

Be a gardener.
Dig a ditch,
toil and sweat,
and turn the earth upside down
and seek the deepness
and water the plants in time.
Continue this labor
and make sweet floods to run
and noble and abundant fruits
to spring.
Take this food and drink
and carry it to God
as your true worship.

*The tender grass grows up at his command to
feed the cattle, and there are fruit trees,
vegetables and grain for man to cultivate,
and wine to make him glad, and olive oil as
lotion for his skin, and bread to give him strength.*

PSALM 104:14–15

ALL THINGS
BRIGHT
AND GOOD

We plow the fields and scatter the good seed on the land,
But it is fed and watered by God's almighty hand;
He sends the snow in winter, the warmth to swell the grain,
The breezes and the sunshine, and soft refreshing rain.

He only is the Maker of all things near and far;
He paints the wayside flower, He lights the evening star;
The winds and waves obey Him, by Him the birds are fed;
Much more to us, His children, He gives our daily bread.

We thank Thee, then, O Father, for all things
bright and good, The seedtime and
the harvest, our life, our health, our food;
Accept the gifts we offer for all Thy love imparts,
And, what Thou most desirest,
our humble, thankful hearts. Amen.

Because the Lord is my Shepherd,
I have everything I need!
PSALM 23:1

Instruction ends in the schoolroom,
but education ends only with life.

**The end of all learning is to know God,
and out of that knowledge
to love and imitate Him.**

*"You are the light of the world. . . . Let your light
shine before men, that they may see your
good deeds and praise your Father in heaven."*
MATTHEW 5:14,16 NIV

May the saddest day of your future be
no worse than the happiest day of your past.

A GRADUATION BLESSING

May God bless you on this day of great achievement. May you be surrounded by the love of family and friends, and may your joy be full in celebration.

May all that you have learned be put to its intended use so that you may fulfill your divine destiny. May your steps be ordered by God as He guides You on the right path. May you be filled with wisdom and insight so that you will excel in your endeavors and prosper in all you do.

May you run the race set before you in health and without lack. May you be blessed with God-ordained relationships to enrich your life's journey. May peace be yours when you are troubled, and may You realize you are never alone for God is always with you. May you be filled with God's love, and may you be a bright and shining light to a world engulfed in darkness. May God shower you with blessings, and may you be crowned with success.

Amen.

Blessings crown the head of the righteous.
PROVERBS 10:6 NIV

If you have good eyesight and good hearing,
thank God who gave them to you.
PROVERBS 20:12

Cultivate the thankful Spirit!
It will be to you a perpetual feast.

I thank thee, God, and like a child
Rejoice as for a Christmas gift,
That I am living—just alive—
Just for this human face I wear,
That I can see the sun, the sea,
The hills and grass and leafy trees,
And walk beneath the host of stars
And watch the lovely moon above.

NAME THEM ONE BY ONE

The cold, dreary morning matched Jean's mood. The single mother had been up most of the night with her sick child and couldn't remember when she'd had a full night's rest. Perhaps it was sleep deprivation that clouded her thoughts. It didn't help that the dishes from the previous night were piled high in the sink, there were mountains of laundry to do, and she had countless other duties on her never-ending to-do list. *There's just not enough of me to go around,* she moaned as her pity party got into full swing. Having to wear all the hats of being both mother and father left her feeling depleted and overwhelmed.

But then little Alexis climbed into her mother's lap, free of the fever from the night before. Her chipper personality was enough to encourage anyone. *Count your many blessings, name them one by one.* The words bubbled up inside Jean. She knew she had much more to be thankful for than to gripe about. Her daughter, for one. Somehow, Alexis made it all worthwhile. As she began recounting other things for which she was thankful, the blessings from God began to overshadow the difficulties, and the sunshine of God's hope began to warm Jean's heart again.

WE THANK THEE

For flowers that bloom about our feet;
For tender grass, so fresh, so sweet;
For song of bird and hum of bee;
For all things fair we hear or see,—
Father in heaven, we thank Thee!

For blue of stream and blue of sky;
For pleasant shade of branches high;
For fragrant air and cooling breeze;
For beauty of the blooming trees,—
Father in heaven, we thank Thee!

For mother-love and father-care,
For brothers strong and sisters fair;
For love at home and here each day;
For guidance lest we go astray—
Father in heaven, we thank Thee!

For this new morning with its light;
For rest and shelter of the night;
For health and food, for love and friends;
For ev'ry thing His goodness sends—
Father in heaven, we thank Thee!

I am convinced that nothing can ever separate us
from his love. Death can't, and life can't.
The angels won't, and all the powers of
hell itself cannot keep God's love away.
ROMANS 8:38

**In His love He clothes us, enfolds and
embraces us; that tender lover completely
surrounds us, never to leave us.
As I see it He is everything that is good.**

As for that which is beyond your strength,
be absolutely certain that our Lord loves you,
devotedly and individually, loves you just as you
are. . . . Accustom yourself to the wonderful
thought that God loves you with a tenderness,
a generosity, and an intimacy that surpasses
all your dreams. Give yourself up with joy to
a loving confidence in God and have courage to
believe firmly that God's action toward you
is a masterpiece of partiality and love.
Rest tranquilly in this abiding conviction.

THE BOOK OF BLESSINGS

A PRAYER FOR THE
BLESSING OF
GOD'S LOVE

*I pray that Christ will be more and more at home in
your hearts, living within you as you trust in him. May
your roots go down deep into the soil of God's marvelous
love; and may you be able to feel and understand, as all
God's children should, how long, how wide, how deep,
and how high his love really is; and to experience this
love for yourselves, though it is so great that you will
never see the end of it or fully know or understand it.
And so at last you will be filled up with God himself.*

EPHESIANS 3:17–19

God loves each of us as if there
were only one of us.

Unconditional love—a rare and precious gift. But even
those who love us most will let us down at some point. It's part
of being human, though most have good intentions. There is
One who will never disappoint you, however. In fact God *is*
love. He loves you more than you can fathom, and He will never
let you down. In fact, there is nothing you could ever do to
change His love for you. Talk about a blessing!

No one ever looks in vain to the Great Physician.

Look to your health; and if you have it, praise
God and value it next to a good conscience;
for health is the second blessing that we mortals
are capable of—a blessing that money cannot buy.

Praise the LORD, O my soul,
and forget not all his benefits—
who forgives all your sins
and heals all your diseases.

PSALM 103:2–3 NIV

Good health is easy to take for granted—until you
lose it! Even if you are sick or suffering from a
disability, there are aspects of your health for which
you can be thankful. Your heart beats without your
thinking about it. Your lungs breathe with little
or no effort on your part. Your digestive system
works on its own. Your body is a miraculous
creation. Thank God for good health today!

A BLESSING FOR HEALTH

May the blessing of health be yours. May God's precious promises for wholeness and healing give you strength and hope to receive.

May you realize that not only does the Lord forgive your sins, but He can heal your diseases. May the example of Jesus healing all who were oppressed with sickness be an encouragement to you as You seek Him.

May quietness of mind and the Lord's peace act as a healing balm to your soul. May the sense of well-being be yours as you rest in the Father's arms and let Him care for you.

May your spirit be healed and made new in Christ, filling you with eternal life.

May good health be yours—spirit, soul, and body.

Amen.

He personally carried away our sins in his own body on the cross so we can be dead to sin and live for what is right. You have been healed by his wounds!

1 PETER 2:24 NLT

In all things of nature there
is something marvelous.

Every creature is a divine word
because it proclaims God.

**The more I study nature, the more
I am amazed at the Creator.**

*"If God cares so wonderfully for flowers
that are here today and gone tomorrow,
won't he more surely care for you?"*
MATTHEW 6:30

God Converses with Us through Nature

The man who can . . . converse with God through
nature finds in the material forms around him,
an inexhaustible source of power and happiness—
like the life of angels. Our highest life and glory is
to be alive to God. When this great awareness
of Him and this power of communion with Him
is carried . . . into the realm of nature, then the
walls of our world are as the gates of heaven.

All nature is within your hands;
you make the summer and the winter too.
PSALM 74:17

God has two dwellings:
one in heaven, and the other
in a meek and thankful heart.

**The favorite place of God
is in the heart of man.**

I am the vase of God,
He fills me to the brim,
He is the ocean deep;
contained I am in Him.

**Fountain of life, and all abounding grace,
Our source, our center, and our dwelling place!**

THE BLESSING OF GOD'S PRESENCE

The greatest blessing you bring to your family
is the presence of God in your life.
The fragrance of His presence sweetens
the atmosphere of your home.
The beauty of His presence
warms the relationships within its walls.
The joy of His presence lightens every heart.
The glory of His presence fills all its chambers
with rare and precious treasures.

We are the temple of the living God. As God has said:
"I will live with them and walk among them, and
I will be their God, and they will be my people."

2 CORINTHIANS 6:16 NIV

*I am come that they might have life, and
that they might have it more abundantly.*

I am the good shepherd.

JOHN 10:10–11 KJV

Every morning the sun rises to warm
the earth. If it were to fail to shine for just
one minute, all life on the earth would die.
The rains come to water the earth. There is
fertility in the soil, life in the seeds, oxygen in
the air. The providence of God is about us
in unbelievable abundance every moment.

**May you live as long as you want,
And never want as long as you live.**

THE BLESSING OF ABUNDANCE

You take care of the earth and water it,
making it rich and fertile.
The rivers of God will not run dry;
they provide a bountiful harvest of grain,
for you have ordered it so.
You drench the plowed ground with rain,
melting the clods and leveling the ridges.
You soften the earth with showers
and bless its abundant crops.
You crown the year with a bountiful harvest;
even the hard pathways overflow with abundance.
The wilderness becomes a lush pasture,
and the hillsides blossom with joy.

PSALM 65:9–12 NLT

Who falls for love of God
shall rise a star.

**Our faults are like a grain of sand beside
the great mountain of the mercies of God.**

*In my prosperity I said, "This is forever; nothing
can stop me now! The Lord has shown me his favor.
He has made me steady as a mountain."*

PSALM 30:6–7

Measure not God's love and favor by your own
feeling. The sun shines as clearly in the darkest
day as it does in the brightest. The difference
is not in the sun, but in some clouds.

A prayer of blessing from the Bible:

*Let the Lord our God favor us and give us success.
May he give permanence to all we do.*

PSALM 90:17

A BLESSING FOR GOD'S FAVOR

May the blessing of divine favor be yours as a child of the living God. May His smile shine upon You as You seek His face. May you experience the comfort and joy of knowing you have been adopted into His family and are greatly favored by Him. May you comprehend that He esteems you just like He esteems His Son because you've been made His child too.

As you greet the world in your everyday life, may the Lord's favor surround you as a shield. May it protect you from those who would do you ill. May you be respected by your family, boss, coworkers, clients, neighbors, and everyone else you encounter. As you walk in God's wisdom and ways, may you excel in your endeavors and have the respect He desires for you.

May divine favor be yours in every way that you need it, and may it bring glory to Him.

Amen.

> *[The LORD's] anger lasts only a moment,*
> *but his favor lasts a lifetime;*
>
> PSALM 30:5 NIV

If God maintains sun and planets
in bright and ordered beauty,
He can keep us.

**God's investment in us is so great
He could not possibly abandon us.**

*Do not fear, for I have redeemed you;
I have called you by name, you are mine.
When you pass through the waters, I will be with you;
and through the rivers, they shall not overwhelm you;
when you walk through fire you shall not be burned,
and the flame shall not consume you.
For I am the LORD your God.*

ISAIAH 43:1–3 NRSV

A LOVELY REMINDER

He could hardly see to drive. "I never thought I'd consider rush hour a blessing," Sam murmured as he battled the elements and the traffic. The layoff notice sat on the seat beside him, seemingly mocking him as he tried to make his way home. In a strange way, it was kind of a relief. The possibility had been hanging over him for months.

What if we lose our house? What if our insurance runs out before I get a new job? What if the children get sick? What if . . . ? What about . . . ? The rapid-fire questions assaulted his mind at the same pace the deluge was hitting the windshield. "I need some music," he finally said out loud. As the inspirational CD played, the car was soon filled with melodies of hope and faith. Sam felt peace settling his mind as he sang along.

Before he knew it, he was pulling in the driveway, and the rainstorm had passed. As he got out of his car, he couldn't help but notice the rainbow in the clouds above his house—a lovely reminder that the same God of the Bible still keeps His promises today.

A PASSAGE OF BLESSING FROM THE BIBLE

Blessings for Those Who Follow God

These are the blessings that will come upon you:
Blessings in the city,
Blessings in the field;
Many children,
Ample crops,
Large flocks and herds;
Blessings of fruit and bread;
Blessings when you come in,
Blessings when you go out.
The Lord will defeat your enemies before you; they will
march out together against you but scatter before you in
seven directions! The Lord will bless you with good crops
and healthy cattle, and prosper everything you do when you
arrive in the land the Lord your God is giving you. He will
change you into a holy people dedicated to himself; this he has
promised to do if you will only obey him and walk in his
ways. All the nations in the world shall see that you belong to
the Lord, and they will stand in awe.

The Lord will give you an abundance of good things
in the land, just as he promised: many children,
many cattle, and abundant crops. He will open
to you his wonderful treasury of rain in the heavens,
to give you fine crops every season. He will bless
everything you do; and you shall lend to many nations,
but shall not borrow from them. If you will only
listen and obey the commandments of the Lord your
God that I am giving you today, he will make you the
head and not the tail, and you shall always have the
upper hand. But each of these blessings depends on your
not turning aside in any way from the laws I have
given you; and you must never worship other gods.

DEUTERONOMY 28:2–14

God delights in blessing
those who obey Him.

Let the sea in all its vastness roar with praise!
Let the earth and all those living on it shout,
"Glory to the Lord."

Let the waves clap their hands in glee, and the
hills sing out their songs of joy before the Lord.
PSALM 98:7–9 TLB

Earth with her thousand voices praises God.

Every formula which expresses a law
of nature is a hymn of praise to God.
—INSCRIPTION ON A BUST IN THE HALL OF FAME

A BLESSING OF NATURE

Nature Praises God

Does not all nature around me praise God? If I were silent, I should be an exception to the universe. Does not the thunder praise Him as it rolls like drums in the march of the God of armies? Do not the mountains praise Him when the woods upon their summits wave in adoration? Does not the lightning write His name in letters of fire? Has not the whole earth a voice? And shall I, can I, silent be?

Nothing is without voice; God everywhere can hear
Arising from creation His praise and echo clear.

Jesus said that though people remain quiet, even the rocks would cry out praise to God. Could it be that the crash of waves on the shore, the wind whistling through the trees, and the songs the birds sing are all shouting God's praises in their own language? Tuning in to the joyful chorus is a blessing indeed!

Walls for the wind,
And a roof for the rain,
And drinks beside the fire—
Laughter to cheer you
And those you love near you,
And all that your heart may desire!
Bless you and yours
As well as the cottage you live in.
May the roof overhead be well thatched
And those inside be well matched.

By wisdom a house is built,
and through understanding it is established;
through knowledge its rooms are filled
with rare and beautiful treasures.

PROVERBS 24:3–4 NIV

A BLESSING ON A NEW HOME

May this new home be more than just a physical house, but rather may it be a home filled with life and love. May it be filled with laughter and good cheer, and may it be a place where good memories are made.

May there be harmony among those who dwell here, and may strife be turned out of doors. May each member of the family honor one another, and may all be treated with respect. May only kind words be spoken here and harsh words never uttered. May it be a place of growth and grace, a happy dwelling place.

May light fill every chamber, and may those who live here be a beacon of hope to draw those who are weary and burdened. May every person who crosses the threshold be met with Your peace and find a safe harbor, a place of refuge. May they leave better than when they arrived, refreshed, and restored.

Amen.

Stand up and bless the LORD your God
for ever and ever: and blessed be thy glorious name,
which is exalted above all blessing and praise.
NEHEMIAH 9:5 KJV

God particularly pours out His blessings upon
those who know how much they need Him.

There are three requisites to the proper
enjoyment of earthly blessings: a thankful
reflection on the goodness of the giver; a deep
sense of our own unworthiness; and a
recollection of the uncertainty of our long
possessing them. The first will make us grateful;
the second, humble; and the third, moderate.

Did you know that just like God can bless you, you
can bless *Him?* Think about how good it feels when
you do something nice for someone and it really touches
their heart. In the same way, when God's blessings
make a difference in your life, just knowing He has
blessed you is reward enough for Him. Why not
really make His day and voice your appreciation!

BLESS GOD FOR BLESSING YOU!

Whenever you get a blessing from God, give it back to Him as a love-gift. Take time to meditate before God and offer the blessing back to Him in a deliberate act of worship. . . . God will never allow you to keep a spiritual blessing completely for yourself. It must be given back to Him so that He can make it a blessing to others.

> *I bless the holy name of God with all my heart.*
> *Yes, I will bless the Lord and not forget*
> *the glorious things he does for me. . . .*
>
> *He ransoms me from hell. He surrounds me with*
> *loving-kindness and tender mercies. He fills my life*
> *with good things! My youth is renewed like the eagle's!*
>
> PSALM 103:1-2,4-5

Dashing in big drops on the narrow pane,
and making mournful music for the mind,
I hear the singing of the frequent rain.

**The daily showers rejoice the thirsty earth,
and bless the flowery buds.**

May the blessing of God's soft rain be on you,
Falling gently on your head,
refreshing your soul
With the sweetness of little flowers
newly blooming.
May the strength of the winds of Heaven
bless you,
Carrying the rain to wash your spirit clean
Sparkling after in the sunlight.

*You sent abundant rain, O God,
to refresh the weary Promised Land.*

PSALM 68:9 NLT

A BLESSING OF NATURE

The Blessing of Rain

It isn't raining rain to me,
It's raining daffodils;
In every dimpled drop I see
Wild flowers are on the hills.
The clouds of gray engulf the day
And overwhelm the town;
It isn't raining rain to me,
It's raining roses down.

It isn't raining rain to me,
But fields of clover bloom,
Where any buccaneering bee
Can find a bed and a room.
A health unto the happy,
A fig for him who frets!
It isn't raining rain to me,
It's raining violets.

*I will make them and the places round about my hill
a blessing; and I will cause the shower to come down
in his season; there shall be showers of blessing.
And the tree of the field shall yield her fruit, and the
earth shall yield her increase, and they shall be safe
in their land, and shall know that I am the LORD.*

EZEKIEL 34:26–27 KJV

Finding, following, keeping, struggling,
Is He sure to bless?
Saints, apostles, prophets, martyrs,
Answer, "Yes."

For all the blessings of the year,
For all the friends we hold so dear,
For peace on earth, both far and near,
We thank Thee, Lord.

For life and health, those common things,
Which every day and hour brings,
For home, where our affection clings,
We thank Thee, Lord.

Give thanks in all circumstances, for this
is God's will for you in Christ Jesus.
1 THESSALONIANS 5:18 NIV

I prayed for this child, and the LORD has granted me what I asked of him. So now I give him to the LORD. For his whole life he will be given over to the LORD.

1 SAMUEL 1:27–28 NIV

A prayer of blessing from the Bible:

May the God of your ancestors help you;
may the Almighty bless you
with the blessings of the . . . breasts and womb.

GENESIS 49:25 NLT

What does peace *look* like? Just take a peak at the expression on your little one's face while sleeping. What does peace *sound* like? Listen to the gentle breathing with the rise and fall of your wee one's chest. What does peace *smell* like? Nothing can compare to the lovely scent of a freshly bathed baby. What does peace *feel* like? Any mother will tell you that some of the most peaceful and fulfilling moments in life have come while holding and rocking their babies.

Babies are indeed a blessing from God.

A BLESSING FOR PARENTS AND THEIR NEW BABY

May you and your newborn baby be blessed as you embark on your lifelong relationship with one another. May you be equipped with everything you need to be good parents. May you be filled with love and be quick to forgive. May you not be easily angered, but may you be patient and kind. May you discipline fairly and not provoke your child to anger. May you have wise answers when you need them and stay flexible as your child grows and changes. May you be given insight into your child's destiny, and may you know what to do to equip your child to fulfill that plan. May the atmosphere in your family be one of acceptance with open communication, and may your home be filled with laughter as you enjoy one another.

May your child thrive under your care and grow up to be wise and responsible. Instead of being rebellious, may your child be obedient and teachable. May healthy friendships throughout life keep your child on the right path. May your little one be healthy, happy, and safe.

Amen.

God sets the lonely in families.
PSALM 68:6 NIV

Where love reigns, the very joy
of heaven itself is felt.

A prayer of blessing from the Bible:

*May God who gives patience, steadiness, and
encouragement help you to live in complete
harmony with each other—each with
the attitude of Christ toward the other.*
ROMANS 15:5 TLB

A happy family is but an earlier heaven.

THE BLESSING OF
THE FAMILY

Civilization varies with the family, and the family with civilization. Its highest and most complete realization is found where enlightened Christianity prevails; where woman is exalted to her true and lofty place as equal with the man; where husband and wife are one in honor, influence, and affection, and where children are a common bond of care and love. This is the idea of a perfect family.

> *How very good and pleasant it is*
> *when kindred live together in unity! . . .*
> *For there the LORD ordained his blessing,*
> *life forevermore.*
> PSALM 133:1,3 NRSV

A prayer of blessing from the Bible:

*May our Lord Jesus Christ himself and God our
Father, who has loved us and given us everlasting
comfort and hope which we don't deserve,
comfort your hearts with all comfort.*

2 THESSALONIANS 2:16-17

**God does not love us because we are valuable.
We are valuable because God loves us.**

Can we not understand that God, who is love,
who is even made out of love,
simply cannot help blessing us.
We do not need to beg Him to bless us;
He simply cannot help it.

*It was through reading the Scripture that I came to
realize that I could never find God's favor by trying—
and failing—to obey the laws. I came to realize that
acceptance with God comes by believing in Christ.*

GALATIANS 2:19

THE TRANSFORMING POWER OF GOD'S LOVE

The hot tears streamed down her face. Christy couldn't control their flow as she pulled out of her mother's driveway. *I'll never be good enough*, she concluded. Now in her thirties, Christy still felt like a little girl seeking her mother's approval. And with each negative encounter, the pain grew more intense.

It had always been difficult. The two women seemed locked in a vicious cycle—Christy yearning for approval, her mother pushing her away. *It's not her fault*, Christy reasoned. Her mother had never received the nurturing she needed either. The pattern firmly established, Christy was beginning to realize that she had been setting herself up for disappointment.

Turning to her Bible when she arrived home, her eyes fell upon Jeremiah 31, "I have loved you with an everlasting love." The words were like a healing balm to Christy's wounded soul. *I will never disappoint you or turn you away*, she sensed the Father saying to her. The more she pondered the blessing of God's great love for her, the more His love eclipsed the pain.

Her mother hadn't changed, but Christy experienced a turning point that day. She began seeking God for the acceptance her soul craved, and bit by bit His love began to transform her.

THE ETERNAL GOODNESS

I bow my forehead to the dust,
I veil mine eyes for shame,
And urge, in trembling self-distrust,
A prayer without a claim.

I see the wrong that round me lies,
I feel the guilt within;
I hear, with groan and travail-cries,
The world confess its sin.

Yet, in the maddening maze of things,
And tossed by storm and flood,
To one fixed trust my spirit clings;
I know that God is good! . . .

I know not what the future hath
Of marvel or surprise,
Assured alone that life and death
His mercy underlies.

And if my heart and flesh are weak
To bear an untried pain,
The bruised reed He will not break,
But strengthen and sustain.

No offering of my own I have,
Nor works my faith to prove;
I can but give the gifts He gave,
And plead His love for love.

And so beside the Silent Sea
I wait the muffled oar;
No harm from Him can come to me
On ocean or on shore.

I know not where His islands lift
Their fronded palms in air;
I only know I cannot drift
Beyond His love and care.

THE BLESSING OF FREEDOM FROM FEAR

Don't be afraid, for I am with you. Do not be dismayed, for I am your God. I will strengthen you. I will help you. I will uphold you with my victorious right hand.

ISAIAH 41:10 TLB

Our Lord cannot endure that any who love Him should be worried, for fear is painful. Thus St. John says: "Love casts out fear." Love cannot put up with either fear or pain, and so, to grow in [understanding of His] love is to diminish in fear, and when one has [responded and] become a perfect lover, fear has gone out of him altogether.

Courage is fear that has said its prayers.

[God] has said, "I will never leave you or forsake you." So we can say with confidence,
"The Lord is my helper;
I will not be afraid.
What can anyone do to me?"

HEBREWS 13:5–6 NRSV

A BLESSING FOR A CHILD'S FIRST DAY OF SCHOOL

May God bless and keep you, my child, as you embark on your first day of school. May you see it as an exciting adventure and not as a thing to be dreaded or feared. May God make His peace and His presence known to you, filling you with confidence and joy.

May your teacher be sensitive to your needs and be given wisdom as to how to bring out the best in you as well as the other children in your class. May she be given the patience and strength she needs to do her job well, and may she be blessed for her efforts.

May Godly children be brought into your life, and may you be kept from children and influences that would lead you astray. May God's angels watch over you to keep you safe at all times, and may all of your steps be guided by Him. May goodness and mercy follow you today and all the days of your life.

Amen.

"A woman giving birth to a child has pain because
her time has come; but when her baby is born
she forgets the anguish because of her joy
that a child is born into the world."

JOHN 16:21 NIV

Of all the joys that lighten suffering earth,
what joy is welcomed like a newborn child?

A babe in the house is a well-spring
of pleasure, a messenger of peace and
love, a resting place for innocence on
earth, a link between angels and men.

A sweet new blossom of humanity, fresh fallen
from God's own home, to flower on earth.

Living jewels, dropped unstained from heaven.

A BABY IS A BLESSING

*When it was time for Elizabeth to have her baby,
she gave birth to a son. Her neighbors and
relatives heard that the Lord had shown
her great mercy, and they shared her joy.*

LUKE 1:57–58 NIV

The first handshake in life is the
greatest of all: the clasp of an infant
around the finger of a parent.

**Baby: Unwritten history!
Unfathomed mystery!**

The birth of every new baby is God's
vote of confidence in the future of man.

The first and most important thing we know
about God is that we know nothing about
Him except what He himself makes known.

**As prayer is the voice of man to God,
so revelation is the voice of God to man.**

A prayer of blessing from the Bible:

*May [you] be filled with the full (deep and clear)
knowledge of His will in all spiritual wisdom
[in comprehensive insight into the ways and
purposes of God] and in understanding
and discernment of spiritual things.*

COLOSSIANS 1:9 AMP

Remember what it was like in math class when
that little light came on inside your head and you
finally understood how to work the problem?
God reveals His truth in much the same way.
As you ponder a passage of Scripture, invite
Him to reveal His truth to you. That same little
light will come on as God's Word comes alive
and you discover answers—not to math problems,
but for the very problems you encounter every day.

THE BLESSING OF GOD AND HIS TRUTH REVEALED

A prayer of blessing from the Bible:

May you have grace and peace from . . . Jesus
Christ who faithfully reveals all truth to us.

REVELATION 1:4–5

God hides nothing. His very work from the
beginning is revelation—a casting aside of veil,
a showing to men of truth after truth. On and
on from fact divine He advances, until at length
in His Son, Jesus, He unveils His very face.

A prayer of blessing from the Bible:

May [God] grant you a spirit of wisdom and revelation
[of insight into mysteries and secrets] in the [deep and
intimate] knowledge of Him, By having the eyes of your
heart flooded with light, so that you can know and
understand the hope to which He has called you, and
how rich is His glorious inheritance in the saints.

EPHESIANS 1:17–18 AMP

Every revelation of truth felt with interior
savor and spiritual joy is a secret whispering
of God in the ear of a pure soul.

Whenever I bring clouds over the earth and the
rainbow appears in the clouds, I will remember
my covenant between me and you and all living
creatures of every kind. Never again will
the waters become a flood to destroy all life.
GENESIS 9:14–15 NIV

My heart leaps up when I behold
A rainbow in the sky.

O, beautiful rainbow, all woven of light!
Heaven surely is open when thou dost
appear, and bending above thee the angels
draw near, and sing "The rainbow—
the rainbow; the smile of God is here!"

A rainbow is heaven's promise
in Technicolor.

A BLESSING OF NATURE

The Blessing of a Rainbow

Rainbows would never be rainbows,
If sunshine had never met rain.
No one would ever need comfort,
If there were no sadness and pain.
But life holds both sunshine and shadows,
The days aren't all bright and fair—
So look through the shower for the rainbows
You'll always find hope shining there.

A prayer of blessing from the Bible:

May the God of hope fill you with all joy and peace
as you trust in him, so that you may overflow
with hope by the power of the Holy Spirit.
ROMANS 15:13 NIV

Drop thy still dews of quietness,
Till all our strivings cease;
Take from our souls the strain and stress,
And let our ordered lives confess
The beauty of thy peace.

**Solitude, though it be silent as light, is
like light, the mightiest of agencies.**

A prayer of blessing from the Bible:
*May blessing and peace of heart be your
rich gifts from God our Father,
and from Jesus Christ our Lord.*
1 THESSALONIANS 1:1 TLB

Peace and quiet is a rare commodity in today's
busy world, especially if you have kids in the
house. But instead of savoring the solitude when
you can get it, do you instinctively flip on the TV or
radio, out of habit if not for any other reason? The
next time you are home alone or everyone else is
asleep, tune in to the quiet that surrounds you and
bask in the peace that the blessing of quiet brings.

THE BLESSING OF QUIET

At the heart of the cyclone tearing the sky
And flinging the clouds and the towers by,
Is a place of central calm;
So here in the roar of mortal things,
I have a place where my spirit sings,
In the hollow of God's palm.

**With an eye made quiet by the power
Of harmony, and the deep power of joy,
We see into the life of things.**

Be still, and know that I am God.
PSALM 46:10 NIV

I will go before thee, and make
the crooked places straight.
ISAIAH 45:2 KJV

We never attempt the resources of God
until we attempt the impossible.

Nothing before, nothing behind;
The steps of faith
Fall on the seeming void, and find
The rock beneath.

May the road rise to meet you.
May the wind be always at your back
May the sun shine warm upon your face
And the rain fall soft upon your fields
And until we meet again
May God hold you in the palm of His hand.

A BLESSING FOR A YOUNG PERSON GOING OFF TO COLLEGE

As you begin this new chapter of your life, may you be filled with courage and a sense of adventure for the great things God has in store for you. May you be aware of His presence, for He will never leave you, and may you be shielded from harm and evil influences. May you be free of fear, but filled with peace to guard your heart and mind. May you seek God, for He longs to bless you, and may His angels watch over you to keep you safe.

May your time at college be everything you have hoped for and then some. May you learn more about yourself and receive insight as to God's good plan for you. May you set wise goals to help you measure your progress, and may you be encouraged by each accomplishment. May you learn all you need to learn, meet all the people you are destined to meet, and be filled with joy as you continue on your journey.

Amen.

Knowledge is folly unless grace guides it.

The best things are nearest:
breath in your nostrils, light in your eyes,
flowers at your feet, duties at your hand,
the path of God just before you.

Blessings we enjoy daily, and for the
most of them, because they be so common,
men forget to pay their praises. But let
not us, because it is a sacrifice so pleasing
to Him who still protects us, and gives us
flowers, and showers, and meat, and content.

Oh, that men would give thanks
to the LORD for His goodness,
And for His wonderful works to the children of men!
For He satisfies the longing soul,
And fills the hungry soul with goodness.

PSALM 107:8–9 NKJV

THANKFULNESS REVEALS BLESSINGS

If one should give me a dish of sand, and tell me there were particles of iron in it, I might look for them with my eyes, and search for them with my clumsy fingers, and be unable to detect them; but let me take a magnet and sweep through it, and how would it draw to itself the almost invisible particles by the mere power of attraction. The unthankful heart, like my finger in the sand, discovers no mercies; but let the thankful heart sweep through the day, and as the magnet finds the iron, so it will find, in every hour, some heavenly blessings, only the iron in God's sand is gold!

Give thanks to the Lord, for he is good;
his loving-kindness continues forever.

PSALM 136:1

THE BLESSING OF FORGIVENESS

So now there is no condemnation for those who belong
to Christ Jesus. For the power of the life-giving
Spirit has freed you through Christ Jesus.
ROMANS 8:1–2 NLT

In the Bible there are three distinctive meanings
of grace: it means the mercy and active love of
God; it means the winsome attractiveness of God;
it means the strength of God to overcome.

Grace can pardon our ungodliness and justify
us with Christ's righteousness; it can put the
Spirit of Jesus Christ within us; it can help
us when we are down; it can heal us when
we are wounded; it can multiply pardons, as
we through frailty multiply transgressions.

If we confess our sins to him, he is faithful and just
to forgive us and to cleanse us from every wrong.
1 JOHN 1:9 NLT

A BLESSED REVELATION

Jacob wished he could take a vacation from the anger in his soul, and the shower provided some temporary relief as the hot water washed over him. Life had dealt Jacob some serious blows, and it was only natural that he was angry. Yet as a believer, he knew that forgiveness was the only way out of his emotional prison. The kicker was that no matter how hard he tried to forgive, the negative feelings always returned, as faithfully as a boomerang. The resulting guilt only added to his defeat.

As he focused on the cathartic effect of the shower, it dawned on him that forgiving is a process similar to taking a shower. *Just because I shower once doesn't mean I will never have to again. Likewise, when negative emotions return after I've forgiven, it doesn't mean that I haven't forgiven. It just means I have to forgive again.*

It wasn't the total solution, but the revelation served as a turning point for Jacob. At least now instead of feeling guilty for recurring negative emotions, he knew what to do with them. He was confident that if he stayed committed to forgive, God would be faithful to bring lasting healing.

The winter is past, the rain is over and gone.
The flowers are springing up and the time of
the singing of birds has come. Yes, spring is here.
SONG OF SOLOMON 2:11–12 TLB

Springtime . . . invites you to try out
its splendor . . . to believe anew. To realize
that the same Lord who renews the trees
with buds and blossoms is ready to
renew your life with hope and courage.

Think of the number of trees and blades
of grass and flowers, the extravagant
wealth of beauty no one ever sees!
Think of the sunrises and sunsets we never
look at! God is lavish in every degree.

A BLESSING OF NATURE

The Blessing of Spring

The Year's at the spring
And the day's at the morn;
Morning's at seven;
The hillside's dew-pearled;
The lark's on the wing;
The snail's on the thorn:
God's in his heaven—
All's right with the world!

Ah, spring. What a glorious blessing after
a long, cold winter! It's a wonderful time
of new beginnings, of refreshing, and
rejuvenation. Is there an area of your life
where you could use a fresh start? Regardless
of the date on the calendar, why not declare
that spring has sprung in that area and
invite God to give you the lift that you need.

If you don't get everything you want, think
of the things you don't get that you don't want.

Every misery I miss is a new blessing.

Never look at what you have lost;
look at what you have left.

**Reflect upon your present blessings of which
every man has many; not on your past
misfortunes of which all men have some.**

For some reason, it is easier to see the glass
half empty rather than half full. Perhaps it's
human nature. The good news is that it doesn't
have to stay that way! There will always be
things we wish were different, but we can turn
the tide by focusing on the good things we so
easily take for granted. Take time to actually
enjoy some of those things. You'll be glad
you did, and that glass might start to look full!

ENJOY YOUR
BLESSINGS

A person who is to be happy must
actively enjoy his blessings.

**God always gives his very best to those
who leave the choice with Him.**

If you discern [God's] love in every moment
of happiness, you will multiply a thousandfold
your capacity to fully enjoy your blessings.

*You have granted him eternal blessings
and made him glad with the joy of your presence.*

PSALM 21:6 NIV

[Jesus] replied, "Blessed rather are those
who hear the word of God and obey it."
LUKE 11:28 NIV

The Lord gives His blessing when
he finds the vessel empty.

**The greatest blessing we ever get from God
is to know that we are destitute spiritually.**

Did you know that Jesus *loves* to bless you?
Many hold the view that He is a hard
taskmaster who imposes harsh demands on
His followers. But just the opposite is true.
He said His yoke is easy, His burden light.
And so we wouldn't have to go it alone, He even
sent the Holy Spirit to help us whenever
we need it. Enjoy His blessings today!

A PASSAGE OF BLESSING FROM THE BIBLE

Jesus Blessed His Disciples Before He Ascended

*When [Jesus] had led [the disciples] out to the
vicinity of Bethany, he lifted up his hands and
blessed them. While he was blessing them,
he left them and was taken up into heaven.
Then they worshiped him and returned to
Jerusalem with great joy. And they stayed
continually at the temple, praising God.*

LUKE 24:50–53 NIV

Jesus departed from our sight that
He might return to our heart.
He departed, and behold, He is here.

A prayer of blessing from the Bible:

*May the Lord make your love to grow and overflow
to each other and to everyone else, just as our love
does toward you. This will result in your hearts
being made strong, sinless and holy by God
our Father, so that you may stand before him
guiltless on that day when our Lord Jesus
Christ returns with all those who belong to him.*

1 THESSALONIANS 3:12–13 TLB

Marriage has in it less of beauty, but more
of safety, than the single life; it has more care,
but less danger; it is more merry, and more
sad; it is fuller of sorrows, and fuller of joys;
it lies under more burdens, but it is supported
by all the strengths of love, and charity,
and those burdens are delightful.

A BLESSING FOR
A HUSBAND
FROM HIS WIFE

I thank God for bringing you into my life. May He richly bless you and cause you to fulfill your destiny. May you grow in wisdom and understanding, so that in all situations you know the right thing to do. May your mind be filled with creative ideas, making the world be a better place because you are in it. May all your efforts be crowned with success, and may you receive promotion and financial reward as you diligently pursue your career.

May God give you strength to overcome adversity. May you be healthy and live a long life. May you be kept from temptation and protected from your enemies. May you be delivered from all harm.

May our relationship be all God means for it to be. May you understand servant leadership as you direct our household, and may we flow together as one. May we be sensitive to each other's needs, always putting the other first, and may we encourage one another, always building each other up.

May our companionship be rich and our love like the finest of wines, growing better with each passing year. May our marriage be a bit of heaven on earth.

Amen.

God's rarest blessing is,
after all, a good woman.

Your marriage is more than a sacred covenant
with another person. It is a spiritual discipline
designed to help you know God better, trust
Him more fully, and love Him more deeply.

*Enjoy life with the woman whom you love all
the days of your fleeting life which He has given
to you under the sun; for this is your reward in life.*
ECCLESIASTES 9:9 NASB

*The man who finds a wife finds a good thing;
she is a blessing to him from the Lord.*
PROVERBS 18:22

A BLESSING FOR A WIFE FROM HER HUSBAND

May you be blessed for being such a blessing to me. May you be empowered to fulfill God's plan for your life, and may He fill you with His wisdom as you approach each role that you fill.

May you know how much I admire you and appreciate what you bring to our marriage. May I be the husband you need me to be, and may our relationship satisfy your needs for romance and intimacy.

May your role as a mother be filled with joy as you watch our children grow up. As they take their place in the world, may you witness abundant fruit from your faithful nurturing and training.

May you be blessed with friends, both old and new, and may you enrich one another in those relationships. May you experience success in your career, and may you have opportunities to exercise your areas of expertise. May you receive promotion as you continue to grow in the special gifts God has given the world through you.

May peace surround you to shield you from anxiety and stress. May you be filled with joy and receive the desires of your heart.

Amen.

*[The LORD] determines the number of the stars
and calls them each by name.*

PSALM 147:4 NIV

Silently one by one, in the infinite
meadows of heaven,
Blossomed the lovely stars, the
forget-me-nots of the angels.

*Praise him, sun and moon,
praise him, all you shining stars. . . .
for he commanded and they were created.
He set them in place for ever and ever.*

PSALM 148:3,5-6 NIV

In wonder-workings, or some bush aflame,
Men look for God and fancy Him concealed;
But in earth's common things
He stands revealed
While grass and flowers and
stars spell out His name.

Stars arise, and the night is holy.

A BLESSING OF NATURE

The Blessing of Stars

If the stars should appear one night in a thousand years, how would men believe and adore; and preserve for many generations the remembrance of the city of God which had been shown! But every night come out these envoys of beauty, and light the universe with their admonishing smile.

Those who are wise will shine like the brightness of the heavens, and those who lead many to righteousness, like the stars for ever and ever.
DANIEL 12:3 NIV

Stars: blessed candles of the night.

There's music in the dawning morn,
There's music in the twilight cloud,
There's music in the depth of night,
When the world is still and dim,
And the stars flame out in the pomp of light,
Like thrones of the cherubim!

YOU ARE BLESSED WITH GOD'S FRIENDSHIP

God and man exist for each other and
neither is satisfied without the other.

**We pursue God because, and only
because, He has first put an urge
within us that spurs us to the pursuit.**

It is God's will that we believe that we see Him
continually, though it seems to us that the sight
be only partial; and through this belief He makes
us always to gain more grace, for God wishes
to be seen, and He wishes to be sought, and He
wishes to be expected, and He wishes to be trusted.

**Prayer of Augustine of Hippo:
My soul is too small to
accommodate You. Enlarge it.**

THE BLESSING OF TIME WITH GOD

Ray stepped a little harder on his brakes than he meant to. Traffic was heavy. Thankfully the driver behind him seemed aware of his surroundings. Tammy and the kids were out of town for another week. He was headed home to a quiet, dark house. He smiled a little at the thought of the fanfare he normally received when he opened the front door.

Anna, Jacob, and Holly would squeal with delight, "Daddy, Daddy, you're home!" Ray recalled always having to drop his briefcase—and anything else in his hands—in order to collect them all into his arms. His heart warmed at the thought.

Just as they anticipate your return home, I anticipate your time with Me, sounded in Ray's heart. There was no need to be blue because of his family's absence. Someone special was waiting for him. And Ray knew he could embrace God's presence without even getting out of the car.

"Look! I have been standing at the door, and I am constantly knocking. If anyone hears me calling him and opens the door, I will come in and fellowship with him and he with me."

REVELATION 3:20

A prayer of blessing from the Bible:

May God's blessings surround you.
COLOSSIANS 4:18

A prayer of blessing from the Bible:

May rich blessings from our Lord
Jesus Christ be with you, every one.
1 THESSALONIANS 5:28

I was a stricken deer that left the herd
Long since; with many an arrow deep infixed
My panting side was charged, when I withdrew
To seek a tranquil death in distant shades.
There was I found by One who had himself
Been hurt by the archers. In his side he bore,
And in his hands and feet, the cruel scars.
With gentle force soliciting the darts,
He drew them forth, and healed and bade me live.

Moses and Aaron Bless the People

*The Lord said to Moses, "Tell Aaron and his sons that
they are to give this special blessing to the people of Israel:
'May the Lord bless and protect you; may the Lord's face
radiate with joy because of you; may he be gracious to you,
show you his favor, and give you his peace.' This is how
Aaron and his sons shall call down my blessings upon the
people of Israel; and I myself will personally bless them."*

NUMBERS 6:22–27

*With hands spread out towards the people, Aaron
blessed them and came down from the altar. Moses and
Aaron went into the Tabernacle, and when they came
out again they blessed the people; and the glory of the
Lord appeared to the whole assembly. Then fire came
from the Lord and consumed the burnt offering and
fat on the altar; and when the people saw it, they all
shouted and fell flat upon the ground before the Lord.*

LEVITICUS 9:22–24

God is good, and he loves goodness;
the godly shall see his face.

PSALM 11:7

In the end, the good will triumph.

Real goodness does not attach itself merely to
this life—it points to another world. Political
or professional reputation cannot last forever,
but a conscience void of offense before
God and man is an inheritance for eternity.

Surely goodness and love will follow me
all the days of my life,
and I will dwell in the house of the LORD
forever.

PSALM 23:6 NIV

THE BLESSING OF GOODNESS

When godliness is produced in you from the life that is deep within you—then that godliness is real, lasting, and the genuine essence of the Lord.

That which is striking and beautiful is not always good, but that which is good is always beautiful.

The heart of a good man is the sanctuary of God.

We must first be made good before we can do good; we must first be made just, before our works can please God. When we are justified by faith in Christ, then come good works.

*Moses inspected the work and saw that they
had done it just as the LORD had commanded.
So Moses blessed them.*

EXODUS 39:43 NIV

Never undertake anything for which you wouldn't
have the courage to ask the blessings of heaven.

**Four steps to achievement:
Plan purposefully, prepare prayerfully,
proceed positively, pursue persistently.**

Doing becomes the natural overflow
of being when the pressure within is
stronger than the pressure without.

A BLESSING FOR A NEW ENDEAVOR

May this new endeavor be blessed, and may it be a blessing to many. May things go smoothly and not be chaotic, and may there be peace instead of stress. May there be love instead of strife and unity instead of discord, and may all the needs of the enterprise be met so that there will be no lack.

May just the right people come forward to fill the necessary positions, and may they be given wisdom to fill their roles. May the leaders make good decisions, and may those who carry out those decisions be willing and positive in their attitudes. May creative ideas flow freely, and may there be open minds. May everything be done with excellence, and may there be corresponding reward. May this endeavor be blessed in every way.

Amen.

God is a God of new beginnings, and He loves to get in on the ground floor of new ventures. Since He is *the* Creator, why not invite Him to get involved? You might be surprised at some of the bright ideas that suddenly begin to dawn on you and others in your organization.

How precious to me are your thoughts, O God!
How vast is the sum of them!
Were I to count them,
they would outnumber the grains of sand.

PSALM 139:17 NIV

God hugs you.

See, I have engraved you on the palms of my hands;
your walls are ever before me.

ISAIAH 49:16 NIV

Just as birds, wherever they fly,
always meet with the air, so we,
wherever we go, or wherever
we are, always find God present.

THE BLESSING THAT GOD THINKS ABOUT YOU

It is but right that our hearts should be on God,
when the heart of God is so much on us.

God carries your picture in His wallet.

From the very beginning, you have been on
His Mind. He never stops thinking about you—
even while you sleep at night, even when
you're busy doing other things you are on
God's mind. You may forget Him,
but He never stops delighting in you.

**So necessary is our friendship to God that he
approaches us and asks us to be His friends.**

The light [of the Bible] is like the body of heaven
in its clearness; its vastness like the bosom
of the sea; its variety like scenes of nature.

**There is a hint of the everlasting
in the vastness of the sea.**

Mystery of waters, never slumbering sea!
Impassioned orator, with lips sublime,
whose waves are arguments to prove a God.

**The ocean's surfy, slow, deep, mellow
voice is full of mystery and awe.**

*The seas have lifted up, O LORD,
the seas have lifted up their voice;
the seas have lifted up their pounding waves.
Mightier than the thunder of the great waters,
mightier than the breakers of the sea—
the LORD on high is mighty.*
PSALM 93:3–4 NIV

A BLESSING OF NATURE

The Blessing of the Sea

Frothing foam and lazy roar,
Strength concealed amid wheeling gulls,
Polished shells, and children's
water–splashing feet;
How much you are like Him who gently treats
His creation with such tenderness.

Secret life of fish and plant
Hidden beneath the weighty deep,
Hidden yet in a secret dance of ebb and flow,
To those who diligently seek, you show
His face.

We only see a little of the ocean,
A few miles distance from the rocky shore;
But oh! Out there beyond—
beyond the eyes' horizon
There's more—there's more.

He who appoints the sun
to shine by day,
who decrees the moon and stars
to shine by night,
who stirs up the sea
so that its waves roar—
the LORD Almighty is his name.

JEREMIAH 31:35 NIV

He alone stretches out the heavens
and treads on the waves of the sea. . . .
He performs wonders that cannot be fathomed,
miracles that cannot be counted.

JOB 9:8,10 NIV

A SEASIDE BLESSING

Beth had always loved the ocean. After thirty years of returning each summer, she still experienced a thrill at the first sight of water. The roar of the waves hitting the beach and the smell of the salt air were miraculous in their therapeutic effect.

But would they work their wonders this time? The stress from Beth's job had taken its toll on her body, her teenage son's drug addiction had broken her heart, and now her marriage was in trouble. Life had become a cyclone swirling around her at a breakneck speed.

As she sat on the balcony overlooking the water, the steady rhythm of the waves breaking on the shore had their usual calming effect. *Have you ever thought that these same waves have been breaking continually for many thousands of years?* She sensed God speaking to her heart. *I see to it that they never cease. If I can control the waves and keep the earth spinning on its axis, am I not able to handle your circumstances?*

Beth could sense her spirits lifting. Nothing outwardly had changed, but she could breathe a little easier, aware that the God of the universe was at work in her life.

All work and no rest takes the spring
and bound out of the most vigorous life.
Time spent in judicious resting is
not time wasted, but time gained.

There are pauses amidst study, and even pauses
of seeming idleness, in which a process goes on
which may be likened to the digestion of food.
In those seasons of repose, the powers are
gathering their strength for new efforts; as land
which lies fallow recovers itself for tillage.

*By the seventh day God had finished the work
he had been doing; so on the seventh day he rested
from all his work. And God blessed the seventh
day and made it holy, because on it he rested
from all the work of creating that he had done.*
GENESIS 2:2–3 NIV

THE BLESSING OF REST

Renewal and restoration are not luxuries. They are essentials. Being alone and resting for a while is not selfish. It is Christ-like. Taking your day off each week or rewarding yourself with a relaxing, refreshing vacation is not carnal. It's spiritual. There is absolutely nothing enviable or spiritual about a coronary or a nervous breakdown, nor is an ultra-busy schedule necessarily the mark of a productive life.

Jesus knows we must come apart and rest
awhile, or else we may just plain come apart.

*"Come to me and I will give you rest—all of you
who work so hard beneath a heavy yoke. Wear
my yoke—for it fits perfectly—and let me teach you;
for I am gentle and humble, and you shall find rest
for your souls; for I give you only light burdens."*
MATTHEW 11:28-29

A FINAL BLESSING

The LORD bless you, and keep you;
The LORD make His face shine on you,
And be gracious to you;
The LORD lift up His countenance on you,
And give you peace.

Index of Blessings

ACKNOWLEDGMENTS

Irish Blessing (7a,40c,54b,64,68c,90c), Author Unknown (8a,10ab,18b,24,30c,32a,53,83a,86c,87,120a), Joseph Addison (8b), Aristotle (8c,50a), Charles Kingsley (9), Johnson Oatman Jr. (12-13), Dallas Willard (15), Marcus Valerius Martial (16a), Jean Paul Richter (16b), Konrad von Gesner (18a), G.I. Liland (19), Henry Vaughan (20a), Dorothy Frances Gurney (20b), Robert Browning (21,97), George Lillo (22a), Charles R. Swindoll (22b,96a,123a), Mildred C. Letton (25), Gale Heide (26a), Mrs. Charles Cowan (28), Joseph Hart (29), George Washington Carver (30a), McCandlish Phillips (30b), Virginia Wuerfel (31), James C. Dobson (32b), Charles Dickens (34a,98d), Johann Wolfgang von Goethe (34b), Pope John Paul II (34c), J.R. Lowell (34d), Billy Graham (35), Chinese Proverb (36a), Ethel Percy Andrus (36b), Margaret Gordon Kuhlman (37), Julian of Norwich (38,46,108c), Matthias Claudius (39,42b), F.W. Robertson (40a), John Milton (40b), John R. MacDuff (42a), Ralph Waldo Emerson (44-45,107a), Julian of Norwich (46a), Abbe Henri de Tourville (46b), Augustine of Hippo (47,101,108d), F.F. Bosworth (48a), Izaak Walton (48b,52a,92b,98b), Bonaventure (50b), Louis Pasteur (50c), G.B. Cheever (51), Jewish Proverb (52b), Angelus Silesius (52c,63b), Madame Jeanne Marie de La Mothe Guyon (52d,113a), Charles L. Allen (54a,94a), Ben Jonson (56a), Jean Baptiste Marie Vianney (56b), Richard Sibbs (56c), F.B. Meyer (58a,90b), Erwin W. Lutzer (58b), Samuel Taylor Coleridge (62a), Maria Mitchell (62b), Charles Haddon Spurgeon (63a), Robert Harold

Schuller (66a,98c), Hannah More (66b), Oswald Chambers (67,96b), W.H. Burleigh (68a), Matthew Prior (68b), Robert Loveman (69), John Mason Neale (70), Baptist Hymn (71), Hannah Hurnard (74a), John Bowring (74b), William Aikman (75), Archbishop Fulton J. Sheen (76a), Hannah Whitall Smith (76b), John Greenleaf Whittier (78–79,88a,90b), Meister Eckhart (80a,117d), Dorothy Bernard (80b), Caroline Norton (82a), Martin Farquhar Tupper (82b), Gerald Massey (82c), Channing Pollock (82d), Josiah Gilbert Holland (83b), Imogene Fey (83c), Heinrich Emil Brunner (84a), John Henry Newman (84b), George Macdonald (85a), Walter Hilton (85b), William Wordsworth (86a,89b), Sarah J. Hale (86b), Thomas de Quincey (88b), Edwin Markham (89a), George Herbert (91), Robert Louis Balfour Stevenson (92a), Henry Ward Beecher (93), John Bunyan (94b), Oscar Wilde (98a), Cicero (99a), James Hudson Taylor (99b), Frances J. Roberts (99c), Jeremy Taylor (102), George Meredith (104a), Gary Thomas (104b), Henry Wadsworth Longfellow (106ac), Minot Judson Savage (106b), William Shakespeare (107b), William Hone (107c), A.W. Tozer (108ab,117c), William Cowper (110), Euripides (112a), Daniel Webster (112b), Ninon de L'Enclos (113b), Anne–Louise–Germaine de Sta'ebl (113c), Hugh Latimer (113d), Georg Christoph Lichtenberg (114a), William Arthur Ward (114b), Lois Lebar (114c), Hildegarde of Bingen (116a), Francis de Sales (116b), Richard Baxter (117a), Tony Campolo (117b), Cardinal John Henry Newman (118a), J.B. Phillips (118b), Robert Montgomery (118c), Thomas C. Haliburton (118d), Maria Thusick (119), M.B. Grief (122a), J.W. Alexander (122b), Vance Havner (123b).

Additional copies of this title are available
from your local bookstore.

If you have enjoyed this book,
or if it has impacted your life,
we would like to hear from you.

Please contact us at:

Honor Books
An Imprint of Cook Communications Ministries
4050 Lee Vance View
Colorado Springs, CO 80918
www.cookministries.com